HOW TO PRAY

E. Stanley Jones

HOW TO PRAY

E. STANLEY JONES

With commentary by Tom Albin

UPPER
ROOM BOOKS®
NASHVILLE

HOW TO PRAY

LIBRARY OF CONGRESS CATALOGING-IN-PUBLICATION DATA
Jones, E. Stanley (Eli Stanley)l, 1884–1973.
  How to pray / by E. Stanley Jones;—The Upper Room edition / with commentary by Thomas R. Albin.
     pages cm
  ISBN 978-0-8358-1378-5 (print)—ISBN 978-0-8358-1379-2 (mobi)—ISBN 978-0-8358-1380-8 (epub)
1. Prayer—Christianity. I. Albin, Thomas R. II. Title.
  BV215.J66 2015
  248.3'2—dc23

2014030549

CONTENTS

FOREWORD

If I had one gift, and only one gift, to make to the
Christian Church, I would offer the gift of prayer, for
everything follows from prayer.

—E. Stanley Jones

How to Pray was first published in 1943. The
efficacy of Jones's words has continued through
the decades, still speaking clearly and powerfully
today. I feel honored to provide commentary on
the original content. In the following pages you
will find the original text along with my reflec-
tions and suggestions for deeper exploration of
some of Brother Stanley's main points. My reflec-
tions and suggestions fall at the end of each sec-
tion of *How to Pray* and are set in an italic font.
I want to help readers move from information to
transformation, from insight to application. We all
may know about prayer, but do we actually pray?
Reading and study offer means to gain information and understanding; reflection and spiritual
practice can lead to transformation and spiritual
maturity.

E. Stanley Jones deeply desired that men and women, girls and boys, come to understand and experience the unique person and presence of Jesus Christ—in and through the life-transforming practice of prayer. This is my desire as well.

I feel confident that Brother Stanley would agree that people can learn to pray; and, in reality, the Holy Spirit is the teacher. May this book become for you a means of grace—a way to understand and experience God in Christ with the help of the Holy Spirit. My confidence rests on a promise from Jesus Christ:

> I tell you the truth: it is to your advantage that I go away, for if I do not go away, the Advocate will not come to you; but if I go, I will send him to you. . . . When the Spirit of truth comes, he will guide you into all the truth. . . . He will take what is mine and declare it to you. All that the Father has is mine. For this reason I said that he will take what is mine and declare it to you (John 16:7, 13-15).

—Tom Albin
Dean of Upper Room Ministries

INTRODUCTION

The family of E. Stanley Jones is grateful to Upper Room Books for republishing Jones's inspiring small book *How to Pray*, surely a message for this and for all times. Jones writes from deep experience, from prayer experience. He spent two hours each day in prayer, one in the morning and one in the evening. No one and nothing distracted him from this daily communication with God. Jones did not believe in prayer as an optional subject in the curriculum of living but rather the only required subject. He writes the following in *Victorious Living: 364 Daily Devotions*.

> The first discipline must be to establish the prayer habit. . . . Don't fool yourself into saying that you don't need the particular time and place, that you will find God all the time and everywhere. If you are to find God all the time, you must find God some time; and if you are to find God everywhere, you will have to find God somewhere. That sometime and somewhere will be the special prayer time and the special prayer place. (Week 9, Wednesday)

How to Pray offers practical teaching steps in creating a daily habit of prayer at "some time" and "somewhere" as you align your will to God's will, hear God's word for you, and experience God at work in your life.

The commentary of the Rev. Tom Albin, the Dean of Upper Room Ministries, graces this book. Tom also currently serves as the executive director of the North American Christian Ashrams, a spiritual transformation movement created by E. Stanley Jones in India and now worldwide in its influence and impact. (See www.Christianashram. org). He understands that prayer flows from our natural desire for a relationship with God and that the resulting prayer is a life-transforming, two-way communication.

Reading this book will introduce (or reintroduce) you to E. Stanley Jones, a twentieth-century prophet who preached more than sixty thousand sermons in his lifetime, authored twenty-eight books and innumerable articles. His "open secret" was Jesus Christ, the word of God become flesh. A personal relationship with Christ can begin with prayer! We invite you on this journey.

—**Anne Mathews Younes, EdD, DMin**
President, The E. Stanley Jones Foundation
Granddaughter of E. Stanley Jones

For more information about Jones, visit the E. Stanley Jones Foundation website:

www.estanleyjonesfoundation.com

The foundation is dedicated to preserving and extending the legacy of Jones who blessed millions of people around the work with his preaching, teaching, and prolific written works proclaiming Jesus as Lord!

1

WHAT PRAYER REALLY IS

When the disciples make the following request of Jesus, "Lord, teach us to pray," they utter one of the deepest and most universal cries of the human heart. People of all ages have instinctively felt that prayer is the distilled essence of religion. If we know how to pray, we know how to be religious; if not, then religion becomes a closed book. With no effective prayer life, the heart of religion ceases to beat; religion becomes a dead body of forms, customs, and dogmas.

Yet how few Christians (including many ministers) have an effective prayer life! If I were to put my finger on the greatest lack in American Christianity, I would unhesitatingly point to the need for an effective prayer life among laity and clergy.

If I had one gift, and only one gift, to make to the Christian Church, I would offer the gift of prayer, for everything follows from prayer. Prayer tones up the total life. I find by actual experience

I am better or worse as I pray more or less. If my prayer life sags, my whole life sags with it; if my prayer life goes up, my life as a whole goes up. To fail here means I fail all down the line; to succeed here means I succeed everywhere.

We win or lose the battle of the spiritual life during our prayer time. Prayer, rather than being an optional subject in the curriculum of living, is a required subject; it is *the* required subject. We do not graduate into adequate human living without it.

We all may feel more or less convinced of the value of prayer; the difficulty comes in the *how* of prayer. In these chapters I attempt to respond to the "how." I propose to begin at the lowest rung of the ladder so that no one will feel as if I begin beyond him or her.

- Breathe the prayer "Lord, teach me to pray" as you begin the quest for a prayer life. Bathe your very quest in prayer. It may be dim, shadowy, unreal; but this may be the first tottering step toward spiritual maturity.

- As you begin your quest, you must hold in mind this background of thought about prayer: *The universe is an open universe.* The old concept of the universe as a closed system fixed unalterably by natural law, a system in which nothing but foregone conclusions can happen, is a thing of the past. In its place has come a universe where natural law still reigns—yet amid and through that law you discover possibilities open to initiative. This world of freedom amid law leaves many decisions contingent upon human will. Just as many actions will never take place unless the human will decides to do them, many options that open in prayer will not come to fruition unless we choose to cooperate with God to do them. We enter this world of freedom and possibility when we enter into prayer.

§ Another thought that may serve as background: *Prayer is not only the refuge of the weak; it is the reinforcement of the strong.* The idea that only weak people pray is false. The strongest persons who ever walked our planet prayed. In his first public act Jesus stood on Jordan's banks and as he prayed "the heaven was opened" (Luke 3:21). In his last public act he prayed, "Father, into your hands I commend my spirit" (Luke 23:46). Between that first and last act, prayer saturated his whole life.

Prayer does not exist merely for the weak; it is the strength of the strong. Is the scientist weak who humbly bends his knees to the facts of nature and lets them take him by the hand and lead him into mastery through obedience?

§ Another thought you must hold is this: *Prayer is not bending God to my will but bringing my will into conformity with God's so that God's will may work in and through me.* When you are in a small boat and throw out a boat hook to catch hold of the shore, do you pull the shore to yourself or do you pull yourself to the shore? Prayer is not bending the universe to your will, making God a cosmic bellhop for your purposes; prayer is cooperating with God's purposes to do things you never dreamed you could do. The highest form of prayer comes in Jesus' words in Gethsemane: "Yet, not my will but yours be *done*" (Luke 22:42). Jesus did not say, "Your will be borne," which is how we often translate it. He said, "Your will be done," which implies a cooperation with an outgoing, redemptive will that desires our highest good.

§ *Prayer is not an occasional exercise to which you turn now and then; it is a life attitude.* It is the will to cooperate with God in your total life. It reflects an attitude rather than an act. You cannot expect God to come into the occasional if you refuse God in the continuous. Therefore, I am not impressed with the slogan "There are no atheists in foxholes." If people pray only when in foxholes, then prayer becomes a means of getting out of a hole—foxholes or other kinds—but plays no part in a life program. Once out of the foxhole, the pray-er probably takes over on his or her own and dismisses God.

❧ *Prayer, then, is primarily and fundamentally surrender.* When asked to define prayer, Toyohiko Kagawa, a twentieth-century Japanese Christian reformer, rightly replied, "Surrender." You surrender your purposes, your plans, and your will into the hands of God to work them out. But surrender does not mean weak negativism. Prayer constitutes the surrender of the wire to the dynamo, of the flower to the sun, of the student to the processes of education. The Gulf Stream will flow through a straw provided the straw is aligned to the Gulf Stream and not at cross purposes with it.

You as an individual surrender to God and then—shall I say it?—God surrenders to you; divine power lies at your disposal. You work with a mighty purpose, and an almighty purpose works with you.

❧ *Prayer is secondarily assertion.* After you have surrendered to God's will, you can assert your will within that will. Thomas Henry Huxley, a British biologist and educator of the twentieth century, wrote,

> Science seems to teach in the most unmistakable terms the Christian conception of entire surrender to the will of God. Science says, Sit down before the facts as a little child, be prepared to give up every preconceived notion, be willing to be led anywhere

the facts will lead you or you will know nothing.

That is the first attitude of science—humble surrender to the facts. The second attitude involves bold assertion and an assumption of mastery within those facts.

Two attitudes combine—surrender and assertion. The two have to be together: If you only surrender, you are weak; if you only assert, you are weak. But if you are surrendered and then assertive, you are really strong. You will be a positive and creative person because you are surrendered to the will of God.

You are beginning the adventure of cooperation with God. Prayer is exactly that—cooperation with God.

The image of a toddler learning to walk and growing toward physical maturity emphasizes a significant spiritual truth. Jesus spoke of the need to be born again, that is, born of the Spirit, to help us realize that the spiritual life resembles human life and development. As a newborn child has the potential for speech and the desire to communicate, so each of us has the potential and the desire to communicate with God—which is the essence of prayer. As we enter into the attitudes and

practices Jones suggests above, we will learn to pray by allowing the Holy Spirit to teach us, day by day, week by week.

Just as the relationship between parent and child is reciprocal and creative, our relationship with the Creator of the world, the universe and the cosmos involves both reciprocity and creativity. Believe and pray with the knowledge and confidence that all things are possible. Without God, we cannot. Without us, God will not. Together we grow, mature, and flourish.

———

Think again of a child in relation to a loving parent. The parent desires the very best for the child. A willful, rebellious child refuses the love and guidance offered. The child finds life difficult and does not flourish. On the other hand, a child who willingly surrenders his or her will to the guidance of a loving parent will discover more love, more joy, more power and blessing than the he or she could ever imagine. Prayer is the ultimate act of surrender to God.

———

Brother Stanley understood the will of God as our best choice if we are wise enough to perceive it. Surrender to God's love frees the human spirit for joyful obedience and infinite creativity. We need not struggle or strive.

Surrender and trust free us to pray with joy and confidence. As we open ourselves to the deep, life-giving relationship of prayer, we do so with the confidence and great expectation that the promised Holy Spirit will teach us to pray.

2

THE TIME AND PLACE
FOR PRAYER

Now that I have put a background behind prayer, you are in a position to take the first positive steps in the art of creating an effective prayer life.

§ Begin with the environment, the surroundings where you will learn to pray. Make them as favorable as possible. Every home should hold a sacred place, perhaps a place curtained off, into which you can enter to keep your appointment with God. In that sacred place set out the symbols that will help you achieve the prayer mood.

   If you cannot arrange a sacred place, then go into a place that corresponds to the "prayer closet" of which Jesus spoke, where you will be alone without disturbance.

§ Perhaps neither plan is possible. Then make your own sacred place by your power of inward withdrawal. Learn to "shut the door" even amid conditions that would otherwise bring disturbance.

Relaxing physically and mentally helps you create a sacred place. It is a psychological fact that you cannot engrave anything on a tense conscious mind. Relaxation is necessary for receptivity. You want your body in a condition in which it is least obtrusive.

Be comfortable but not slouchy. As you enter the prayer period say to your body: "O body of mine, you may be the vehicle through which God may come to me. Be receptive." And then to each part of the body: "My brain, you are now in the presence of God. Let go, and listen. God speaks; God penetrates; God heals. Receive, receive." And to the eyes, weary with looking at a distracting world: "Close and inwardly see nothing except the One into whose presence you have now come." God touches my eyes; they feel rested, calm, and healed. And to the nerves: "O nerves, intelligence department of my being, strained and torn by living in a world of chaos, I now set you to work on the job of reporting better news. Your God comes—comes with the good news of calm, of poise, of resources, of redemption. Open every cell to that healing, to that calm, to that restoration. Receive, receive, receive."

To your sex life say: "O creative part of me, I surrender you to the creator God. When I sublimate your power into other forms—art, poetry, music, creating new hopes, new souls, new life—I can become creative on another level. So I put you at God's disposal. God cleanses; God redirects." And to the whole body: "God is now in every part, untying knotty nerves in gentleness, bathing every brain cell with the divine presence, reinforcing every weak place with strength, healing all your diseases, coordinating all parts and making them into a cooperating whole. Open every door! Give God all the keys."

§ Then say to your soul: "O soul of mine, you are now in the audience chamber of God. You will meet the Most High. God will come, is coming. Let down all the barriers of your inmost being and welcome the Lord. For God is here—now."

§ Remember that you discover the essence of prayer in right relationship with God—not the getting of this thing or that thing. Don't hasten to place requests before God. Let those go for the moment. With an expectant spirit, let God put a finger on anything in your life not fully surrendered to the divine will. If anything not fully open to God's presence surfaces, bring it up honestly and frankly and look at it. If you see lines of disapproval in God's face, let it go. Otherwise that thing will become a barrier that blocks your communion with God.

§ But if nothing comes up, don't conjure up false guilt. Often we think this conjuring up of false guilt is humility. It is not. God is not petty, going around looking for tiny flaws. Rather, God wants to see if you are essentially sound and set in the right direction. Don't become condemned over imaginary guilt.

§ For instance, suppose that while you pray, your mind wanders. Don't become worried over that. Simply take the wandering thought and allow it to lead you back to God.

§ But suppose the wandering thought is not quite so innocent—an impulse of violence or disrespect, for instance. That can be serious, of course, and can block your communion with God—but only if you harbor and hold the thought. If you dismiss it at once, there is no sin in its coming. Thoughts of sin become sinful thoughts only if entertained and given a seat.

I cannot repeat too often the old statement: "You cannot help the birds flying over your head, but you can keep them from building nests in your hair." The fleeting thought does not constitute sin; the harbored thought does. I have a technique of my own in dismissing wrong thoughts: I bat my eyes rapidly. That breaks up the thought; the batting of the eyes demands attention, calling my attention from the evil thoughts. Then in the midst of it I pray, "O God, help me." That lets me gain my mental equilibrium and control. You may have to work out your particular technique for controlling thoughts.

❧ Suppose the interruption of your meditation does not come from within by straying thoughts but from without: people or disturbing events break your focus. Don't let that upset you. Use the interruption. Jesus went across the lake to get away from the multitudes in order to pray. The people ran around the lake, and when he arrived for his prayer time the crowds awaited him. Instead of being angry and upset, "he had compassion on them . . . he began to teach them many things" (Mark 6:34). Later he feeds them, and then "he dismissed the crowd. After saying farewell to them, he went up on the mountain to pray" (Mark 6:45-46). An interruption became an interpretation.

If you are interrupted, let the interruption be an interpretation rather than an irritation. Return to your prayer time as Jesus did. Don't let the interruption keep you permanently from the prayer time. The season of prayer will be richer for the mastery of the interruption, and the interruption will be richer because of the prayer time.

Much of Jesus' life consisted of one interruption after another, but he didn't permit those interruptions to muddle his prayer time. He mastered them so that they contributed to the central purposes of his life. The spirit of his interrupted prayer went into the interruption and made it illustrate his essential spirit.

It may be that you can glory in interruptions as providing opportunities to evangelize the inevitable. The prayer spirit can turn the mosaic of events into a Christian pattern. Prayer combines action and attitude.

§ Suppose the prayer period is not interrupted from without or from within but is simply dull, dry, and unreal. That too should not upset you. Such dry, dead emotional periods come in every married life, but that needn't disturb the fundamental joy of marriage. The marriage remains intact though the glow of it may be absent. Hold steady; the glow will return to your prayer house. Don't give it up just because there is no glow.

Pray by the clock if you cannot pray by the heartbeat. In doing so you will be fixing a prayer habit, even if you don't feel a prayer glow. The habit is getting into your nerve cells and becoming a fixed attitude or disposition. That fact is more significant than the glow. For once you have established a fixed habit, you will discover yourself inwardly set for prayer as a life attitude.

Something is happening to you even amid the lack of the sense of reality, for you are being fashioned into a person who lives by principles rather than pulse beats, by decisions rather than by delights. Prayer is always right, with or without emotional content. If you cannot pray by an inward clock, then pray by the outward clock.

Permit no exceptions in your prayer schedule; exceptions will break down the habit. The prayer practice or habit is the important thing.

Jesus taught his disciples to pray for things as specific as daily bread. The Psalms often reflect statements made to the inner self; for example, "Why, my soul, are you downcast? Why so disturbed within me? Put your hope in God, for I will yet praise him" (Ps. 42:5, NIV). For seven days approach prayer in the manner described above, and assess whether it helps you develop a habit of prayer.

We are Easter people in a Pentecost world. The Holy Spirit is here now. God's Spirit can communicate directly with our spirits because God created us. Receptivity is our choice. We can quench or resist the Holy Spirit, or we can welcome and receive the Holy Spirit. God gives us the power and privilege of choice. What choices are you making in this moment—will you let down your barriers and actively engage in the practices Brother Stanley has provided?

This simple statement "The essence of prayer is right relationship with God" distills Jones's teaching on prayer and the essential truth of the Christian life. Take time to ponder and reflect on what it means to you and your faith community.

The idea of using a "disruptive" person, event, or illness to glorify God is central to the theology and practice of Brother Stanley. Jesus was not exempt from hardship or disruption—and neither are we as his followers. Life in Christ embraces ordinary interruptions and uses them as opportunities to evangelize the inevitable through the spirit and practice of prayer. When has an interruption become an opportunity in your life?

Christians everywhere undergo spiritual dryness and lack of emotion or feeling in prayer. By using the analogy of marriage, E. Stanley Jones conveys the deeper reality of love and experience that comes through commitment. The reality of the marriage relationship and the reality of the relationship with God in and through prayer continue with or without the momentary warmth and satisfaction of good feelings. The existence of commitment and persistence makes possible future moments of joy.

3

THE STEPS OF PRAYER

We are now ready to take the actual steps of prayer; there are nine of them.

1 Decide what you really want.

The *you* is important. It must not be a wayward part of you wandering into the prayer time with no intention of committing yourself to your prayer request. You cannot pray with a part of yourself and expect God to answer, for God hears what the whole of you is saying. God can only give a whole response to a whole request from a whole person. "If you seek me with all your heart, I will let you find me" (Jer. 29:13).

Notice that Jesus often asked supplicants, "What do you want me to do for you?" (Mark 10:51). This is vital; often a sick person asks for wellness while desiring no such thing. The ill person may use the illness or affliction as a life strategy to gain attention and attendance.

My aunt would regularly attend family gatherings, and she always arrived with some malady. The rest of the family buzzed around her in sympathy and service. Although ill, she managed to eat her portion of the big family dinner. Undoubtedly she made the illness her device for drawing attention to herself.

The same thing can happen in the realm of our moral and spiritual life. We pray with a portion of our being for moral and spiritual victory. Saint Augustine, before he became a saint, used to pray, "O God, make me pure but not now." Before my conversion, I would often pray for God to make me good while fearing that God would take me at my word. Actually, I didn't want to be good. So my prayers were never answered—until in a crisis moment when I really wanted to be different! Then and only then did God hear and deliver me.

Perhaps you willingly pray with the whole "you," but the other "you" is not cooperative. Tell God you are willing to be made willing. Offer your unwillingness to God and, with your consent, God will make it into willingness.

> Longing I sought your presence, Lord,
> With my whole heart did I call and pray,
> And going out toward you, I found you,
> Coming to me on the way.

When you see God coming to you on the way, you will find that God is more than halfway to you.

Let me recount the experience of a woman who said at the beginning of our conversation, "We have everything in our home—everything and nothing." Now she has something. She began, "My day pivots around or radiates from the quiet hour. I had a miserable time establishing it. I could not control my thoughts and pray. I even felt for a time that I was doing myself an injustice to keep trying. Then I confined that time to reading my Bible and writing God a letter. In these letters I am stripped of my self-will, and God's will prevails. It is so satisfying. I am trying to catch up on back correspondence. If I mentioned this experience to some of my associates, they would think me insane. But if this is insanity, I readily confess that I love it."

A beautiful sanity resides in the procedure, for the woman expressed herself clearly in letters. She transferred the habit to her dealings with God. Note that she says, "In [them] I am stripped of my self-will, and God's will prevails." The whole person is beginning to talk to God in those letters.

2 Decide whether the thing you want is a Christian thing.

God has shown us in Christ what divine character is like. God is Christlike. God can only act in a Christlike way. God cannot answer a prayer that contravenes divine character.

A woman who was having an illicit relationship with a married man said, " I thought God was going to answer my prayers and give my lover to me." But how could God do that? She had merely read her desires into the heavens, and the answer only echoed her own desires. Her incorrectly ordered moral universe fell to pieces, and she emerged chastened and disillusioned. God cannot reverse the moral universe, which expresses the divine moral nature, to answer a selfish or immoral whim.

Sit down and ask of all your prayers: "Is the thing I want a Christian thing?" And remember that if it is not a Christian thing, it will do us no good to get it, for only the Christian thing is good for us. Ask God to cleanse your prayers as well as you. Prayer is the naked intent stretching out to God.

Jesus said, "If in my name you ask me for anything"—that is, in my character and according to my spirit—"I will do it" (John 14:14). Within the limits of Christ's character, which means within the limits of the moral universe, you are free to ask anything, and God is free to give you anything.

3 Write it down.

The writing of the prayer will probably help you in self-committal. If you write it, you will probably mean it. Committing a thing to writing almost destines me; I can hardly change it afterward. The writing of it will also save you from hazy indefiniteness. You will pray for this and not something else. There will come a time, of course, when you may not need to write things down; they will have written themselves in you. You can then trust yourself to pray the Christian thing. But at the start you would do well to use all the outer helps you can.

Some people employ the method of writing down their sins and failures and then solemnly burning them in a fire to symbolize the burning up of the old self and its ways in the fire of God's love.

Whether the notion of getting rid of something or the notion of getting something motivates you, writing down your request clarifies it.

4 Still the mind.

By stilling the mind you take a step in receptivity. Prayer is pure receptivity in the first stage. "To all who *received* him, . . . he gave power" (John 1:12, emphasis added). If you come to God tense and agitated, you can get little. Let down the bars on your side; there are none on God's.

Receptivity is the first law of the spiritual life and the first law of all life. An organism can give out as much as it takes in and no more. If it hasn't learned to receive, it hasn't learned to live. The woman mentioned above says: "God has done more for me in my one year of receptivity than I have done for myself in all the years of my life."

In the period of stilling the mind I find myself saying over and over, "Oh, God, you've got me." And again and again the answer comes back, "I know it, my child." Then I sense a quiet rest in which I breathe into every fiber of my being the healing grace of God.

The primary focus of stilling the mind is to get God. Everything else follows from there. I seldom ask for things; if I have God, I know I'll get all I need. The stilling of the mind allows God to get at you, to invade you, to take possession of you. God then pours prayers through you—divine prayers, God-inspired and thus God-answered.

Whenever I am about to speak, I ask the audience members to bow their heads in silent prayer. In that silence I always repeat these words of Jesus, "You did not choose me but I chose you. And I appointed you to go and bear fruit, fruit that will last, so that the Father will give you whatever you ask him in my name" (John 15:16). Stilling the mind by the repetition of that verse makes my mind receptive. I am living in the passive voice. Preaching then is not eager straining; it is receptivity ending in release. The speaker no longer serves as a reservoir with a limited amount to give. Rather, the speaker is a channel attached to unlimited resources.

Prayer is like fastening a cup to the wounded side of a pine tree to allow the rosin to pour into it. You are now nestling into the side of God—the wounded side, if you will—and you allow God's grace to fill your cup. You are taking in the very life of God.

"Be still and know," and you will be full. Be unstill, and you will not know; you will remain empty. Now you are ready for the fifth step.

5 Talk with God about your desires.

Notice I say talk *with* God not talk *to* God, for the conversation goes two ways. And the most vital part may be not what you will say to God but what God will say to you. God wants not only to answer your prayer but to make you—make you into the kind of person through whom prayers can be answered. So this prayer episode is part of a process of God-training. God will answer the prayer provided it will contribute in the long run to the making of you.

When you talk with God about your desire, set the prayer in light of that general intent of allowing God to make you the best instrument of divine purpose. God may have to say a lesser no in order to give a higher yes. On the other hand, this prayer may be a part of that higher purpose. If so, then you can talk it over confidently with God. A boldness will take hold of your spirit as you wait in the divine presence.

One morning I awoke at four o'clock coughing my lungs out. I had tried to stagger through an impossible schedule while barely skirting pneumonia. That morning hour seemed decisive one way or the other. I grew desperate and bold and clutched the garment of God and held on and said, "O God, I don't ask for many things. I've wanted you more than things, but I am asking for this. If you don't help me, I'm done for. I can't go on. Help me."

I knew that my prayer moment had registered. The tide turned.

Talk with God about it and talk with the confidence that God is aching to answer that prayer for you if it is in line with the divine purposes for you.

6 Promise God what you will do to make this prayer come true.

Since the conversation is a two-way experience, the accomplishment is also two-way. You and God answer the request together.

At this point be silent to hear God again, and see if any suggestions come to you about your part in answering the prayer. If definite suggestions arise, then promise you will carry them out.

For instance, one morning I prayed that Gandhi might not be allowed to die—to die pleading for the freedom of his country. Immediately, as I became quiet, I realized that I could send a message to the president urging him to intervene and mediate.

The impulses that come out of the prayer time are usually true impulses of the Spirit. Some would say these impulses are of *your* spirit. But those of us who try this two-way living know that you cannot tell where your spirit ends and the Spirit begins. They now flow back and forth into each other.

The Spirit stimulates our spirit into Spirit-led activities. "Who caused his glorious arm to march at the right hand of Moses?" (Isa. 63:12). When Moses lifted his arm, God did likewise—their arms worked together. And what a working together!

Therefore in the silence tell God what you will do to make the prayer become reality.

7 Do everything loving that comes to your mind about it.

The significance of this step resides in its cleansing and clarifying nature. The word *loving* is the password to finding the source of the suggestions that come to your mind. If the suggestion is unloving, it is probably from your subconscious mind and not from the Spirit. The first fruit of the Spirit is love; if the suggestion does not fit with love, then don't do it. Wait for the suggestion that does fit.

If the word *loving* is important, so is the word *do*. God can only will while awaiting your doing. Your doing opens the floodgates of God's doing.

8 Thank God for answering in accordance with the divine will.

God will answer that prayer. No prayers remain unanswered. But God may answer no as well as yes. No is an answer that may lead to a higher yes.

Moreover, the answer may be delayed in order to toughen your fiber. The very persistence in asking

for something over a long period can be one of the
most character-building processes imaginable. The
prayer becomes fixed in a life attitude that can be
the organizing principle around which life revolves.
God may be more concerned that the prayer exists
than that the answer be forthcoming. God often
holds us off to deepen our character so that we will
not be spiritual crybabies if we do not get everything we want and get it at once.

9 Release the whole prayer from your con-
scious thinking.

Don't keep the prayer at the forefront of your
conscious thinking so that it fosters anxiety. Let it
drop into the subconscious mind and work at that
greater depth. Then all you do will find support in
an undertone of prayer, but you will experience
no anxiety. Dismissing your prayer from the conscious mind serves as an act of faith. Having com-
mitted it to God, you leave it and believe that the
best thing possible will come about.

One or two thoughts may help in closing this
brief outline on the practice of prayer:

Prayer is not so much as act as an attitude. The
first Beatitude says, "Blessed are the poor in spirit,
for theirs is the kingdom of heaven" (Matt. 5:3). The
poor in spirit—the renounced, the surrendered in

spirit—have what? The kingdom of heaven! They do not merely belong to the kingdom of God, but the kingdom of God belongs to them! All of its resources support them; they work with almighty power. Therefore, they go beyond themselves in thinking, in acting, in accomplishment. They are ordinary people doing extraordinary things.

The Acts of the Apostles could be called the Acts of the Holy Spirit, for the Holy Spirit took ordinary human nature and heightened powers and insights until ordinary human nature was quite extraordinary. There are no limits to what can be accomplished by a person who does not limit God.

Prayer opens the channels from our emptiness to God's fullness, from defeat to victory. Therefore, pray or be a prey—a prey to your impulses, to the last event, to your surroundings. The person who prays overcomes everything, for the most redemptive fact of the universe prevails—the will of God. To find that will and live by it is to find yourself. Prayer then creates a free person. Those who do God's will actually do their own deepest wills.

This challenge of bringing your true and total self to the prayer experience is no small thing. Halfhearted,

uncommitted prayer lacks integrity and will not receive a response from God who knows us better than we know ourselves and who loves us more than we can possibly comprehend. Are you ready to bring your whole self to God in the relationship of prayer?

The essence of prayer is relationship. As in any human relationship, communication involves both speaking and listening. Jones emphasizes the importance of listening to God in our times of prayer.

As Christians we believe that God created men and women in the divine image for relationship with the divine and to care for creation. (See Genesis 1:26-27.) This ongoing relationship is possible because we gained more in Christ than we lost in Adam. The gift of the Holy Spirit enables all Christians to restore the relationship with God that we were created to enjoy. When you are "born again"—that is, born of the Spirit—you gain spiritual eyes that enable you to see things you have never seen before and spiritual ears that enable you to hear things you have never heard before. These spiritual senses allow you to receive the spiritual promptings needed to be a true disciple of Jesus Christ.

To develop your spiritual potential, consider securing a spiritual mentor, coach, or guide—someone who has more experience in prayer and the Christian life than you do. Prayerfully consider Jones's invitation to learn how to listen to the Holy Spirit and pray in response to the voice and guidance of God.

God created us with a capacity for relationship with God. As we mature spiritually, we hear and understand God's prompting more clearly and more often. We discover joy and freedom in prayer as we grow in our confidence that we are praying and living the will of God.

Letters to God, written prayers, and prayer journals all serve as aids to prayer. See "Keeping a Spiritual Journal" (page 59) for help in beginning the spiritual practice of a prayer journal.

4

PRAYERS BY
E. STANLEY JONES

The Kingdom of God Is among You
Luke 10:27-37

My God, I see that you are a parent to your family. You have made me so that I cannot get along with myself without getting along with the rest of the family. I see I must live by love or live by loss. Help me this day to live by love. Amen.

How God Reveals the Divine Presence
Psalm 19:1-6; Hebrews 1:10-12; 2:6-9

O God, I begin to see that you are coming to me in Christ. He seems to be that personal approach from the Unseen to me. I would not block that approach. I want you, O God, nothing less than you. Are you, Christ, God coming to me, that I may come to you? Then receive me, for I receive you. Amen.

The Morning Quiet Hour

Mark 1:35-36; Acts 10:9; Ephesians 6:18

Dear God, I need your silences like I need physical food. I dedicate myself to them. May I resolve to cut my physical food each time I cut my spiritual intake. Thus soul and body will go up and down together. For I am resolved to employ this practice and to pay the price to do so. Amen

Help Me to Help

Romans 8:1-2; 2 Corinthians 3:16-18; Galatians 5:1

Dear God, how can I express the gratitude my happy soul would tell? "O for a thousand tongues to sing my great Redeemer's praise." Now help me to tell my gratitude not merely in ecstatic praise but in quiet ways of human helpfulness. May I help the next person I meet, and so on through this day. Amen.

Self-centered Is Self-disrupted

Romans 12:3, 10, 16; 13:9-10; James 2:8-9

Dear God, I see that you have written your laws into the texture of my being. How foolish for me to run against those laws and think I can get away with my folly! Forgive me the folly of warring with myself and hence with you. Amen.

Tempests of Emotion

Psalm 34:5; Isaiah 45:22; Mark 9:33-35

Dear God, I do not sail calm seas. I am driven by tempests of emotion. Help me to harness these to the purposes of your kingdom, for unharnessed they drive me to the rocks upon which both I and my relationship with you are broken. I surrender myself and my emotions to you. Amen.

Necessary to You

Romans 8:13-14; 2 Corinthians 6:1-10

O God, am I—I, who thought myself inferior—necessary not only to others, but to you? Then help me never to let you down. Help me humbly to receive from you and humbly to give back to you—a two-way traffic with you! I shall grow as I get and give. I thank you. Amen.

Prayer—My Native Air

Psalms 27:14; 30:2; Luke 11:1; James 5:16

Gracious Christ, teach me to pray. If I fall down in this area, I fall down everywhere—anemia spreads through my whole being. Give me the mind to pray, the love to pray, the will to pray. Let prayer be the aroma of every act, the atmosphere of every thought, my native air. In your name. Amen.

May I Seem Different

1 Corinthians 6:9-11;

O God, I have come into a new world, for a new world has come into me. Help me to live so that people will seem different to me and I will seem different to them. For I am different, and I am so grateful. Amen.

I Shall Die on No Trifling Cross

Romans 15:1-2; 2 Corinthians 5:15; Philippians 2:4

O Christ—I understand. The whole meaning of life is made plain. I am to follow you to no trifling cross but to this decisive cross on which I shall die—die to my own futile self-will in order to live to your will; die to my own petty self in order to live to your free and strong self. Help me then from this moment to discipline my life to your will. Amen.

An Easter Prayer

1 Corinthians 15

O Risen Lord, walk in the garden of my life, and then it will be forever dedicated—forever it will be no place for sin. It is the place of life, eternal life. I am deathless, for my garden is the garden of the Lord. Life lives here. I thank you. Amen.

5

A BRIEF SPIRITUAL BIOGRAPHY
OF ELI STANLEY JONES (1884-1973)

Born in Baltimore, Maryland, on January 3, 1884, Stanley was—in his own words—ordinary. His early years included regular attendance at the Sunday school classes of Frederick Avenue Methodist Church, South. At fifteen, a guest preacher's sermon "convicted" him, and he went forward to the altar desiring

> to give myself to Christ. . . . I fumbled for the latchstring of the Kingdom of God, wanted reconciliation with my heavenly Father, but took church membership as a substitute. . . . I felt religious for a few weeks, and then it faded out and I was back again exactly where I was before. (*A Song of Ascents*, 26)

At seventeen Stan (as he was known to his friends) experienced a true spiritual conversion through the evangelistic preaching of Robert J. Bateman, "a converted alcoholic on fire with God's love." After two days of seeking Christ at the kneeling rail at the conclusion of the evening services, the spiritual transformation came in his own home.

Before going to the meeting I knelt beside my bed and prayed the sincerest prayer I had prayed so far in my life. My whole life was behind that simple prayer: "O Jesus, save me tonight." And he did! A ray of light pierced my darkness. Hope sprang up in my heart. I found myself saying, "He's going to do it." I now believe he had done it, but I had been taught that you found him at an altar of prayer. So I felt I must get to church. . . . I found myself running the mile to the church. . . . I was all eagerness for the evangelist to stop speaking, so I could get to that altar of prayer. When he did stop, I was the first one there. I had scarcely bent my knees when Heaven broke into my spirit. I was enveloped by assurance, by acceptance, by reconciliation. I grabbed the man next to me by the shoulder and said: "I've got it.". . . I had him— Jesus—and he had me. We had each other. I belonged. (*A Song of Ascents*, 22–28)

As he reflected on this transformational experience sixty-six years later, Stanley wrote,

As I rose from my knees, I felt I wanted to put my arms around the world and share this with everybody. . . . This was a seed moment. The whole of my future was packed into it. (*A Song of Ascents*, 28)

Although this response was common in his day, close observation taught Stan that God works uniquely and creatively with each individual.

> I do not mean to imply that there is a standard type of conversion, and my type is the norm. . . . No two are exactly alike, but all manifest an underlying reality. They all seemed to have a feeling of coming home. . . . when you are converted and find Christ, you find yourself, your Homeland. (*A Song of Ascents*, 31–32)

Desire for More

Having been "born again," Stanley found that his desire for God was not satisfied but rather enhanced—in the same way a growing infant requires more of the mother, not less. His mature reflection on this early experience confirmed his long-standing belief that this desire for more of God is human reality, present in all people in all cultures. Therefore, it is universally true and essential to the message of every evangelist.

> I was satisfied to my depths with what I had, but I wanted more. . . . "Not dissatisfied, but forever unsatisfied" became my basic attitude. . . . I saw that conversion was a once-and-for-all and yet an expanding experience to be applied to larger and larger

areas of life. I was on the quest for more, not different, but more. I would be a Christian-in-the-making. (*A Song of Ascents*, 41–42)

The Formational Power of the Small Group

After formative experiences in his local class meeting, Stanley was shaken and distressed because he came very close to falling into sin. He asked for prayer; immediately all the members of the group fell on their knees.

> They lifted me back to the bosom of God by faith and love. . . . My destiny was in the hands of that group. . . .That germ of experience became, I believe, the idea and impulse back of the Christian Ashram movement. (*A Song of Ascents*, 42–43)

In addition to the spiritual power of the class meeting, the young Mr. Jones enjoyed the company of a spiritual guide. That relationship proved so beneficial that he concluded: "nothing can take the place of a personal friendship." In Stanley's case, it was Miss Nellie Logan, a beloved Sunday school teacher and family friend. As Stanley's mother lay dying, she called Miss Nellie and told her, "I'm turning him over to you, for you to take up my vigil of prayer for him." (*A Song of Ascents*, 44)

Poverty and Testing

At the time young Stanley was ready for college, his father lost his job, the family home and the beds they slept on. Poverty was his lived reality; so Stanley went to work selling insurance for a year. He earned enough money to attend Asbury College in Wilmore, Kentucky, and he took this step of obedience to God's call to preach. There, in 1903, Stanley found the experience and learned the spiritual vocabulary to describe the second blessing, a deeper work of the Holy Spirit in the life of the believer.

The holiness tradition taught him to read his Bible and *The Christian's Secret of a Happy Life* by Hannah Whitehall Smith, a Quaker. These spiritual sources guided Jones into deeper experiences of the Holy Spirit and the need for a full surrender of himself to God.

Years later, the mature Jones understood that this new level of conversion did not erase the reality of the human desires related to "self, sex and the herd"; they were simply restored to their rightful place in the created order—cleansed, consecrated and coordinated as good gifts of God.

India, Marriage, and Failure

Following graduation, Stanley Jones anticipated an assignment to Africa; however, the mission board directed him to India. As he prayed for grace and guidance for this new chapter of his life, the Holy Spirit enabled Jones to see that beneath every culture and custom all human beings are one; their needs are one and the same. Every person needs love, acceptance, and a true relationship with God—which was what Jones came to understand as "conversion."

In 1910, E. Stanley Jones married Mabel Lossing, a missionary teacher at the women's college in Lucknow. They moved fifty miles to Sitapur where they made their home for the next forty years. In 1914, their first child, Eunice, was born. The following year Stanley suffered a ruptured appendix that proved to be inoperable. The pain of his illness was compounded by the stress of expanding responsibilities, both at home and in his ministry— his first district had more than one million people. Then he was assigned another and another until he was responsible for four districts in addition to the Methodist Publishing House in Lucknow.

The responsibility, stress, and physical pain proved too much. He was physically and spiritually at a breaking point. Those around him could see his suffering, and he was ordered to return to the United States after eight and a half years on the mission field. When the furlough ended, Jones was still not ready to return to India, but his superiors told him that he should return to work. Shortly after his return to India, his health and spirit failed again. Twice he went to the mountains to recuperate and pray. Observers during this period would have been hard-pressed to believe that this frail man was about to become one of the most effective evangelists of the twentieth century.

Surrender, Healing, and Transformation

At the lowest point of E. Stanley Jones's physical and spiritual life, God came to him.

> God said to me: "Are you yourself ready for the work to which I have called you?" My reply: "No, Lord, I'm done for. I've reached the end of my resources and I can't go on." "If you'll turn that problem over to me and not worry about it, I'll take care of it." My eager reply: "Lord, I close the bargain right here." I arose from my knees knowing I was a well man. (*A Song of Ascents*, 89)

Jones's healing involved far more than physical touch. It embraced the total person—body, mind, and spirit. Jones could now freely explore and appropriate any good, any truth found anywhere, for he now belonged to the Truth—to Jesus Christ.

Readers looking for easy answers and simple prayers that always get an immediate response from God may find the spiritual autobiography of E. Stanley Jones troubling. Some readers find his honesty and vulnerability disturbing at times; his spiritual journey does not fit the pattern of the revivalist or the holiness tradition of his time. Instead, Jones found a way to use his physical, emotional, and spiritual weakness to connect him to a higher power and a more singular mission.

The biblical record of the earliest Christian confession, "Jesus is Lord" became Jones's essential confession of faith. With this affirmation on his lips he had the courage and assurance needed to answer God's call to engage the educational and political leaders of India in significant dialogue through public lectures, round table conversations, and Ashram retreat experiences.

The Man and His Impact

E. Stanley Jones's mission to India began in 1907 at the age of twenty-three under the sponsorship of the Methodist Episcopal Church. His assignment was to serve as the English-speaking pastor of the Methodist Church in Lucknow and to man-

age the Methodist Publishing House. By the end
of the 1930s his preaching ministry had expanded
to Iraq, Palestine, Egypt, other areas in the Middle
East, Burma, Malaya (Malaysia), the Philippines,
China, and Singapore.

During his ministry in India, Dr. Jones came
to realize the value of the ashram practice of taking time away from work to sit at the feet of a
guru. The word *ashram* comes from the Sanskrit:
a means "from" and *shram* means "hard work." So
an ashram is a retreat from hard work under the
tutelage of a teacher. As Jones worked to indigenize
Christianity in India, he established the Christian
ashram movement, modeled on his experiences in
Gandhi's ashram. Jones intended that the ashram
be a group fellowship focused on Jesus that would
operate as a miniature kingdom of God with Jesus
Christ as teacher.

In 1930 Jones began a Christian ashram where
people of all faiths (and of no faith) could come
and sit at the feet of Jesus. Those who entered left
all symbols of rank and title at the door; all were
addressed by their first name and the designation
of brother or sister. The Rev. Dr. E. Stanley Jones
became known as Brother Stanley. The several-day
Christian ashram was undergirded with prayer
twenty-four hours a day. To support people in their

prayer practice during the ashram, Brother Stanley began to write devotional books in the format of one page per day, each day beginning with a title, suggested scriptures for reading, a spiritual reflection or meditation, and a closing prayer of guidance.

By the end of his life, E. Stanley Jones had published twenty-eight books, two of which sold over one million copies. In 1938, *Time* magazine referred to him as "the world's greatest missionary." In the 1964 edition the editors stated that Jones's only peer in international Christian ministry was the Rev. Billy Graham.

Reinhold Niebuhr described E. Stanley Jones as one of the great saints of his time. In 1962 Jones was nominated for the Nobel Peace Prize, and in 1963 Dr. Jones received the Gandhi Peace Prize. He frequently met and corresponded with Presidents Roosevelt and Eisenhower, General Douglas MacArthur, John Foster Dulles, and Japanese emperor Hirohito.

Within his own denominational tradition, E. Stanley Jones was elected bishop in 1928; however, after praying through the night, he withdrew his name the morning after his election. In the larger ecumenical community, the mission boards and leaders of the National Council of Churches regularly consulted Jones.

Jones's early and unwavering support of the Indian Independence movement led to his banishment from India for a period of years. In addition to supporting freedom for India from British rule, Jones also spoke out against and criticized segregation in the United States. Indeed, throughout his long public career, Jones spoke out more frequently and more passionately on the issue of racial prejudice than any other political topic.

E. Stanley Jones had a deep and authentic love for India, the nation and its people. And India loved Brother Stanley as well; many leaders came to refer to him as an adopted son. He was a friend of Mahatma Gandhi and referred to his murder as the greatest tragedy since Jesus' crucifixion. Soon after Gandhi's death in 1947, Jones was asked by his publisher to write a book about their friendship.

In his autobiography, *A Song of Ascents*, Jones speaks of this book's influence on Martin Luther King Jr.:

> I thought that my book *Mahatma Gandhi, an Interpretation* was a failure. It did not seem to dent the Western world with its emphasis on armaments. But when I saw Dr. Martin Luther King, he said: "It was your book on Gandhi that gave me my first inkling of nonviolent noncooperation. . . . We will turn this whole movement

from violence to nonviolence. We will match
our capacity to suffer against the other's capacity to inflict suffering, our soul force against his
physical force; and we will wear our opponents
down with goodwill." (259–260)

Prayer not only sustained Jones but also pulled
him to God. Daily he would listen to God in an
effort to align his desires and will with God's.

In the complex web of innumerable events and
achievements of Jones's long and incredibly active
life, there runs a single, simple thread: his spiritual
transparency. His character reflected the living reality of Jesus Christ so well that it drew others into
intimacy with God.

Prayer is our channel to God. It sustained E.
Stanley Jones throughout his life, and it will sus-
tain us.

KEEPING A
SPIRITUAL JOURNAL

One timeless Christian devotional practice involves keeping a prayer journal or spiritual notebook. Here are a few ideas to help you begin.

Step 1: KNOW that your journal is a sacred and confidential document. It is for your eyes only. At times you may choose to share an insight that came to you through prayer and reflection, but that will be your decision.

Step 2: LAY ASIDE all fears or concerns about writing. My journal has all sorts of words, phrases, pictures, and shapes. It also has colors and doodles. There are some sentences and paragraphs, but it is not a literary project but a place to record insights, thoughts, feelings, and ideas. You will learn what is right for you. The key to spiritual journaling comes in investing some time every day in letting your hands lead you to new insights through a variety of expressions of your thoughts and feelings. Journaling allows you to use both right-brain and left-brain skills.

Step 3: ENGAGE the practice intentionally with a genuine desire to learn. Anne Broyles, a teacher of spiritual journaling, says that the process of writing down your thoughts clarifies them. Often the process of writing itself generates new creative insight. Broyles also reminds us that a spiritual journal helps you track your growth over time. Your fragile memories may not retain meaningful events and experiences. Specific feelings or creative connections you may have had two weeks agoare hard to recall without a written record.

Step 4: PURCHASE a notebook that you can use as your journal. It can be as simple as a spiral-bound notebook or as fancy as a cloth-bound blank book. You will likely want, at minimum, something more permanent than a ring-binder or paper pad. You'll also will a pen or pencil that feels good in your hand.

Step 5: INVITE the Holy Spirit to help you. Each day, begin the daily practice with your journal and pen nearby. Record your insights at anytime. Write anything that comes to you, even if it seems to be off the topic. The process may seem awkward at first. However, it gets easier over time, and its value becomes more apparent.

Step 6: BE CLEAR by dating each page and starting each new day with a new page. The Holy Spirit comes to us in both our conscious and our unconscious experiences, for God is in all of life. Sometimes God's activity seems clear—in a specifically answered prayer, divine intervention in a seemingly impossible situation, inner strength that surfaces at just the right moment. Other times we recognize God's activity only in hindsight—when we take time to reflect on our lives.

Step 7: BE HONEST since writing in your journal is a spiritual discipline. You need not choose your words carefully or worry about what other people will think. Your journal can help you discover the depth of God's love for you and your true identity as a beloved child of God. Guilt, shame, and self-condemnation only get in the way. Journaling leads to further revelation of who you are and who God is in your life. You come to feel the acceptance of the One who created you and who loves you unconditionally. It does not matter if the writing is legible (other than to you) or if the spelling and punctuation are perfect. As a child of God, you have infinite worth. Your words are unique and important. The more you journal, the more comfortable you will be with the process of putting words on paper.

Step 8: BE FAITHFUL to yourself and to your time. Most people benefit by setting a specific time for prayer and spiritual practice. Some of us are morning people and the quiet of the early morning works best. Others are evening people and quiet time in the evening works best. Others can make time in the middle of the day for prayer and reflection. The time is less important than keeping your commitment to this spiritual discipline

A FINAL WORD OF ADVICE: When distractions come (and they always do), don't fight them; simply write them down on a separate piece of paper and then return to your time with God.

Some days it will seem difficult or impossible to pray and reflect; other days, you may look forward to your time with God. This is part of the natural rhythm of our human experience. Jesus is praying for you at this very minute and the Holy Spirit is longing to teach you to pray. You simply need to show up regularly, ready to learn.

We are in this together—you, me, and the Holy Spirit. Lord, teach us to pray!

—Tom Albin

CPSIA information can be obtained
at www.ICGtesting.com
Printed in the USA
FFOW02n1734010617
36227FF